if there would be no light

poems from my heart

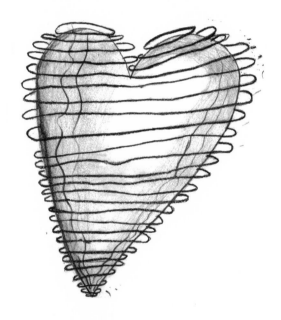

sahara sunday spain

HarperSanFrancisco
A Division of HarperCollins*Publishers*

HarperCollins books may be purchased for educational, business, or sales promotional use. For information please write: Special Markets Department, HarperCollins Publishers, Inc., 10 East 53rd Street, New York, NY 10022.

HarperCollins Web site: http://www.harpercollins.com

HarperCollins®, ▦ ®, and HarperSanFrancisco™ are trademarks of HarperCollins Publishers, Inc.

FIRST EDITION

Library of Congress Cataloging-in-Publication Data
Spain, Sahara Sunday.
    If there would be no light : poems from by heart / Sahara Sunday Spain.
        p. cm.
    ISBN 0–06251740–6 (cloth)
        I. Title.

PS3569.P3377 I35 2000
811'.6—dc21   00–053973

Designed by C. Linda Dingler

01 02 03 04 05 RRD(H) 10 9 8 7 6 5 4 3 2 1

poetry 1998

beautiful love   1999

poems from my heart   2000

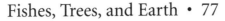

introduction

Sahara Sunday first came into my life through the stories and images brought by her mother, Elisabeth Sunday, when she came to stay with me for a few days. It was like learning of a friend to be, not just the young daughter of a friend. I heard about Sahara's travels with Elisabeth while she pursued her project of photographing spiritual leaders in Africa and Australia, Bali, and India. Sahara created a travel journal from images she made herself, plus stories she asked her mother to write down, and sent it home to friends. She wanted to keep in touch with her classmates at school, nursery school, by sharing experiences. She was three and a half when she started, and published until she was four.

About two years later, Sahara came along with her mother from California to New York, and both stayed with me. This visit coincided with my birthday, so Sahara wrote me a poem and read it to a party of my friends, her poise as great as any one there. When a third friend joined us at my apartment, Sahara chimed in on our grown-up women's conversations when they interested her, and went off into her own six-year-old activities and imagination when they did not. She also danced for us without self-consciousness, and bonded so personally with my other visiting friend that they decided to stay in touch. My friend was sixty. Sahara was six.

When Elisabeth and Sahara came to visit again the following year, I happened to be having dinner with Phoebe Snow, the great singer and song writer, so all four of us spent an evening together. Sahara so impressed Phoebe that she invited her home for the rare honor of meeting her much-loved and profoundly brain-damaged daughter. Sahara treated that daughter with such respect and naturalness that Phoebe spent the next weeks writing a song with Sahara's name as its title, and her spirit as its inspiration.

When Elisabeth and Sahara, then in her eighth year, came for a third visit, Phoebe sang this song to her at the Ms. Foundation for Women's annual benefit. Sahara addressed the large crowd from the stage herself, thus underlining the theme of that year's awards to projects by and for young girls.

I remember thinking: Anyone who's ever met a baby knows there's already a person inside that baby. It's as if each of us were born a daisy or rose or petunia, but then were sometimes made to feel that we should become an iris or lily or daffodil. Somehow, Sahara—thanks to her own spirit plus her loving and creative mother—had managed to stay true to her own unique self, and so to blossom from the beginning.

This year, I've just spoken to Sahara on her ninth birthday. She will be coming to New York to celebrate her first published book, a unique blend of her own images and words. In its pages that you hold in your hands, she tells us to:

> Have compassion and
> forgiveness,
> for people that are lost in their
> minds,
> and can not reach their heart,
> and the love that is held within
> the middle of their heart.

Though she knows the world is not without pain:

> She makes me feel like,
> she's the flower,
> and I'm the dirt,
> and everybody wants to admire,
> the beautiful flower . . .

Sahara remains the rare poet for whom even a river of her tears only makes her decide to become:

> the Goddess of the River

Rain is not an image of sadness:

> Rain drops carry love
> into the world,
> they wash out the things
> that are hurting the earth . . .

As Sahara says:

> Tell me about the beautiful
> experiences that flow in your heart
> and reach your memory.

Thanks to her inspiration, more of us may become our own selves, poets, and artists from the beginning.

Gloria Steinem

poetry

1998

The Flower Girl

There was once a lit-tle girl.
do   re   mi   fa mi- re do

She had flo-wers on her head.
do   re   mi- fa   mi   re   do

She had a be-lov-ed mo-ther,
do   re   mi   fa- so-fa   mi- re

as sweet as a flo-wer bud.
do   re   mi   fa mi- re do.

Time Change

Yesterday is *today,*
and *today* is *tomorrow,*
because *yesterday* changed
places with *today.*

Yesterday is *today*
because *yesterday,* changed into
today which is going to change
into *tomorrow.*

And *today* is *tomorrow* because
yesterday became *today,* so
today will become *tomorrow.*

Sunlight

When the sunlight dances
on the view,
something good
will happen to you.

Giving Heart

I give you my heart.

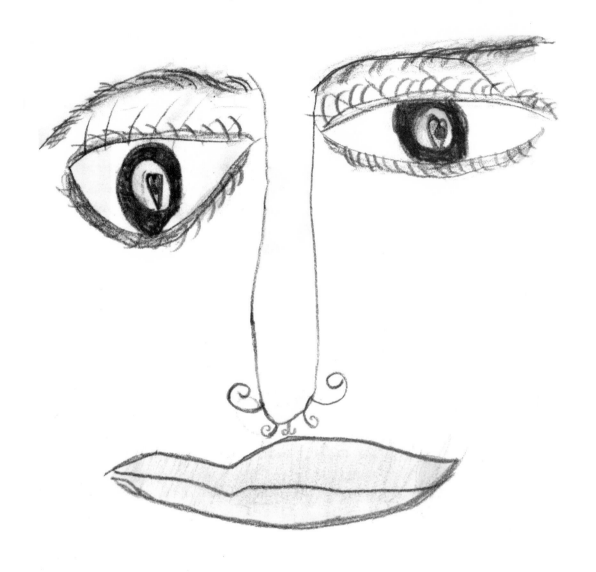

Magic

When I look through your eyes,
I see a disguise,
And in that disguise,
I see love,
And in that love,
You are fabulous.

Trust

You can't trust anybody to take
care of your heart,
unless you know them by heart.

You have to feel confident with
people you know by heart,
or you can assume
they won't turn out to be good in
the end.

You can't assume that people are
taking care of your heart,
if you don't feel confident.

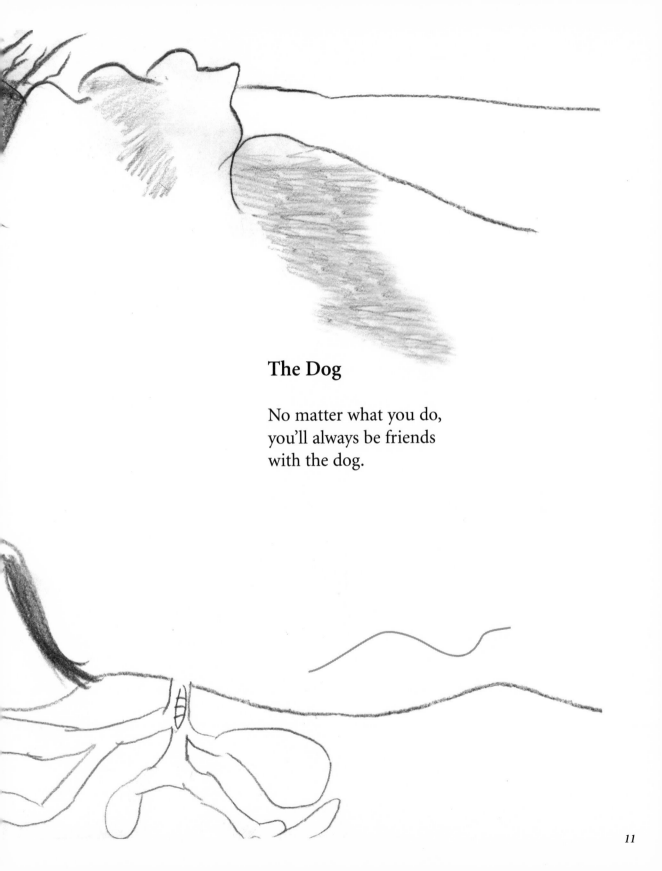

The Dog

No matter what you do,
you'll always be friends
with the dog.

Mother's Milk

When I drink mother's milk,
my heart sweats with love.

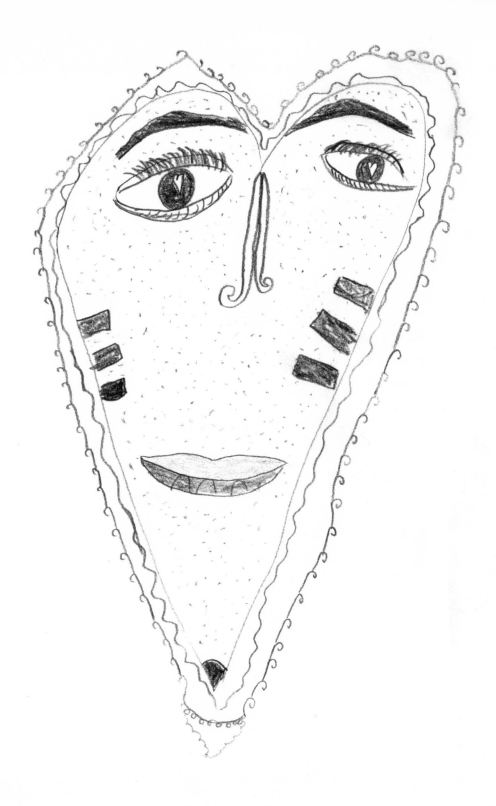

Lost Heart

Have compassion and
forgiveness,
for people that are lost in their
minds,
and can not reach their heart,
and the love that is held within
the middle of their heart.

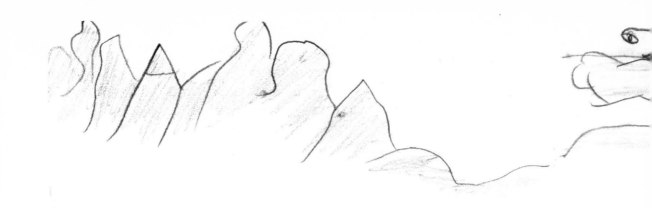

Reincarnation

I believe that everything is
everything
and everybody is every body,
just with a different personality
and in a different form of life.

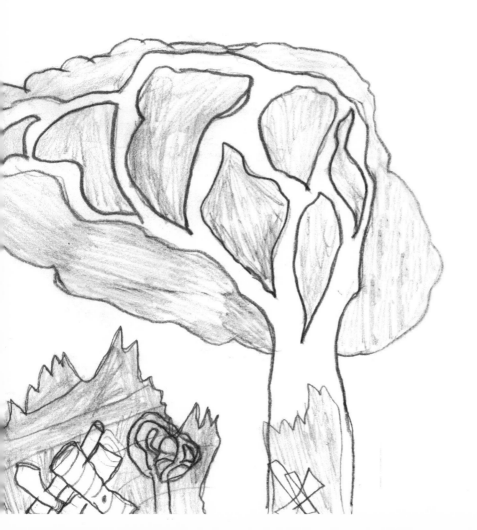

Three Peas in a Pod

Three isn't a bad number if you
are really good friends.

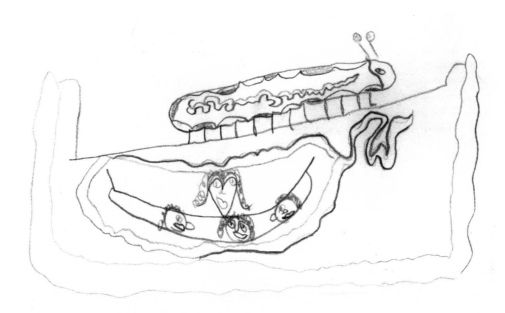

Light of the Mother

Without you, I'm homeless
I'm dark
You're my moon, my stars and
my sun.
I can see my path with you.
You light up the room.

The Love Experience

When you say, "Love,"
You have love streaming through
your body,
So when you love,
everybody loves you,
with the same kind of love,
that you have.

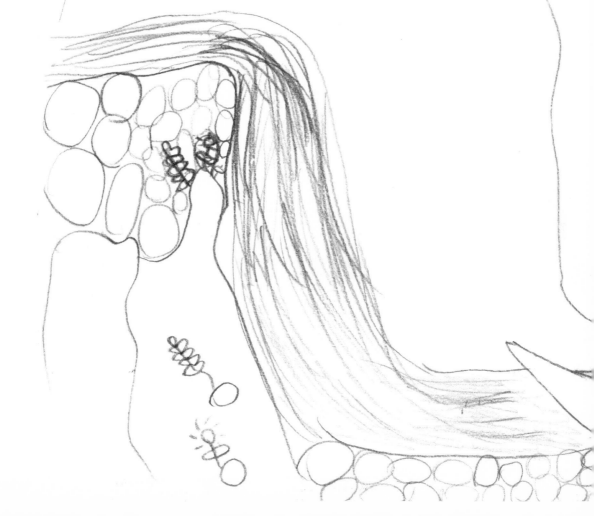

Holy Days

"Holiday" means holy day,
holy day means sacred day.
Everyday is sacred and special,
no matter what,
through all the days in a year.

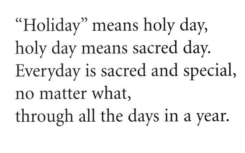

The Sunlight's Hands

In the morning,
the sunlight dances out
everywhere,
but in the night,
the sunlight's hands
bring the rays back,
for the sleep of the beautiful
night.

beautiful love

1999

Mother Nature's Arms

Mother Nature's arms
come bellowing up
from the earth,
and they come make a single tree.

That is how Mother Nature
spreads its air,
and makes the love,
go through all the people,
and all of the animals of Nature.

Things are provided,
food and water from Nature.
How could we hurt it?
We need to help Mother Nature.
Love needs to come upon the
hearts of people.

Weather of Beauty

When it's cloudy,
my heart is happy.
When it's sunny,
my heart is filled with joy.
When the clouds go by,
I pray for them to rain,
because rain is love.

Rain drops carry love
into the world,
they wash out the things
that are hurting the earth,
but mostly,
they carry love into the earth,
and make the love sweat,
upon everybody's body,
like water,
dripping on flowers.

Love, Beauty, Peace, and Air

What air is your favorite love?
What beauty is your favorite peace?
You never told me.

You never told me,
that love could go into peace,
and that beauty could become air.
Because our whole world,
is surrounded by air, love, beauty,
and peace.

Those are the main things that
everybody is surrounded by.

Love forms a circle around you;
and peace adds in,
and air adds in,
and beauty adds in,
and then you become enlightened.

Because all those things form an
enlightened being,
of unknown love.

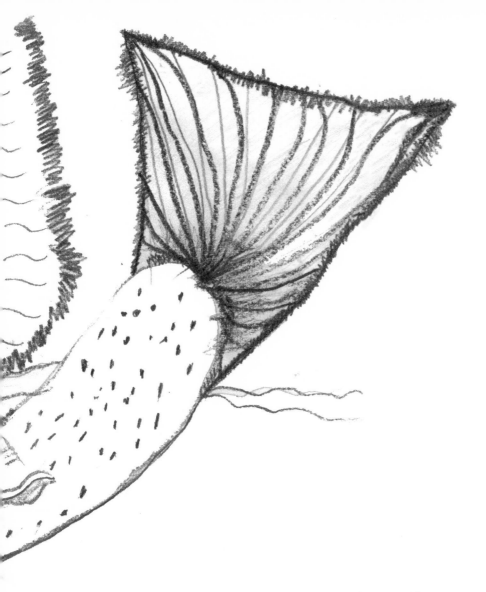

Jumping Fish

Fish jump over the rocks
and out of the water.
They jump to catch the moon
and see the glorious light
coming off of it.

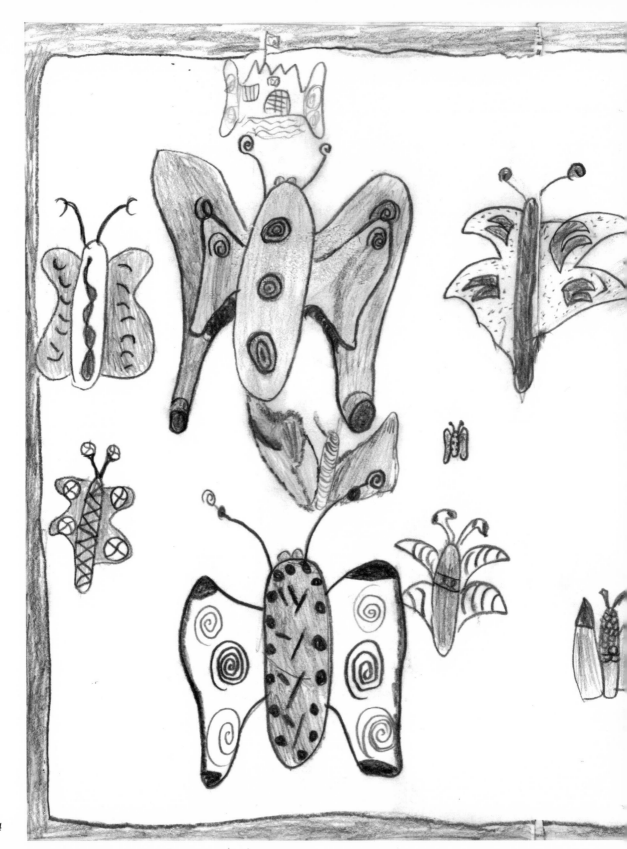

Wings of a Butterfly

You give me wings,
like a butterfly,
dancing with you,
upon two hearts,
together.

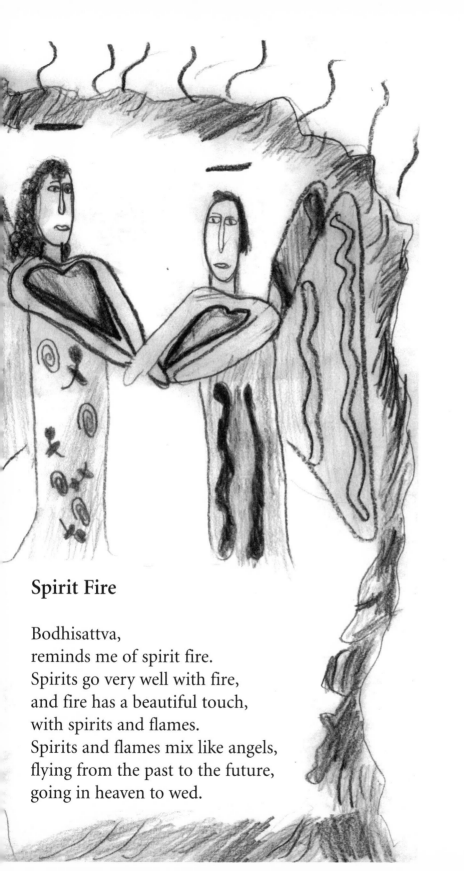

Spirit Fire

Bodhisattva,
reminds me of spirit fire.
Spirits go very well with fire,
and fire has a beautiful touch,
with spirits and flames.
Spirits and flames mix like angels,
flying from the past to the future,
going in heaven to wed.

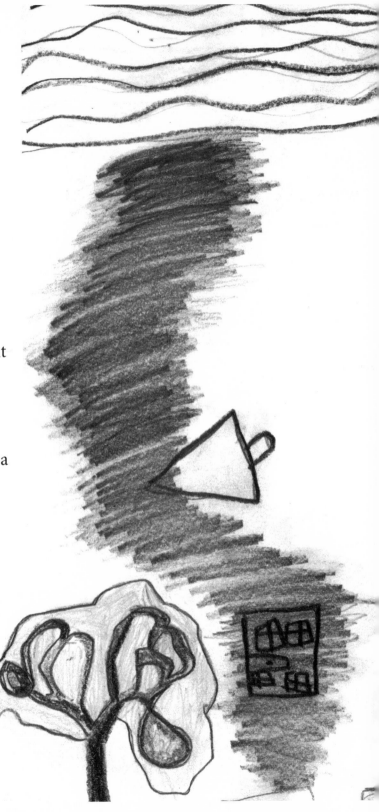

Sad Moments

I feel tears streaming down my
heart and a happy smile on my
face soon fades into a sad moment
of my life.

My heart feels like somebody
pulling the love out of me,
like a tornado sucking a house to a
greenish sky,
that falls to Earth.

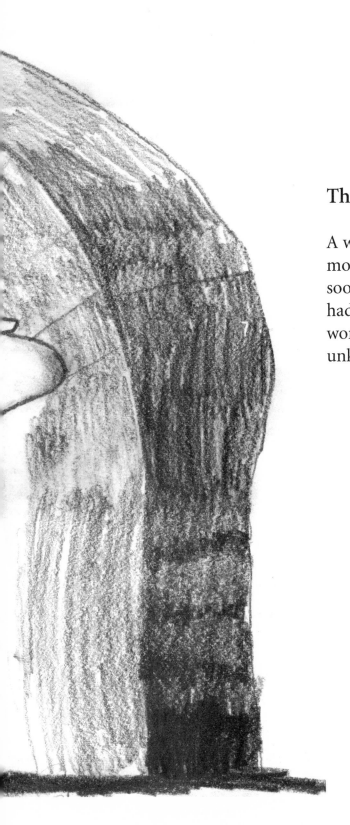

The Unknown Secret

A woman goes into a cave and sees a monster and they both fall in love. As soon as she married the monster and had children, she didn't look like a woman anymore. She looked like the unknown secret.

The Flower and the Dirt

She makes me feel like,
she's the flower,
and I'm the dirt,
and everybody wants to admire,
the beautiful flower,
and nobody
even takes a glance at me,
because I am the dirt,
the dirty dirt.

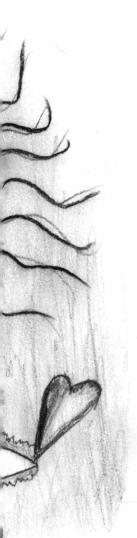

The Love of the World

Together we are a star,
holding a torch,
but it is not an ordinary torch.
Inside this torch is a diamond,
and inside this diamond
is the love of the world.

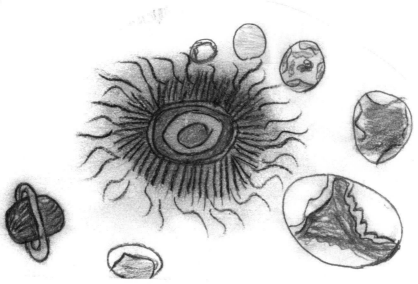

Quick

Quick!
Be an angel walking out of the
light that I see,
before it fades into a silent
darkness.

Fields of Love

When you're in a field
and you say
"love,"
flowers bloom.

Spinner of Life

Spinning life is a spinning wheel,
it spins love into the thread,
which makes the world,
which makes your life.

51

Yaboo

Yaboo

(Yaboo means have love, peace,
beauty and the divine in your
heart.)

Love is Love

Love is love is love,
so love.

Love + love + love = love.

Days of Glory

Tell me about your day.
Tell me what you did.
What was the meaning
of your precious day?

Tell me the days of glory you had.
Tell me about the air and the life
that you experience.

Tell me about the beautiful
experiences that flow in your heart
and reach your memory.

Rare Love

When you have rare love,
your heart is not just in your chest,
it is all over your body.

Love to My Mimi

You put my heart to joy.
You make me sweat with
beautiful love
streaming down my body
like an ocean of pearls.
You inspire my heart with poems.

You're the best that the Gods and
Goddesses brought into life.
They could bring people into life,
but not as beautiful and as
gorgeous and,
spectacular as you.

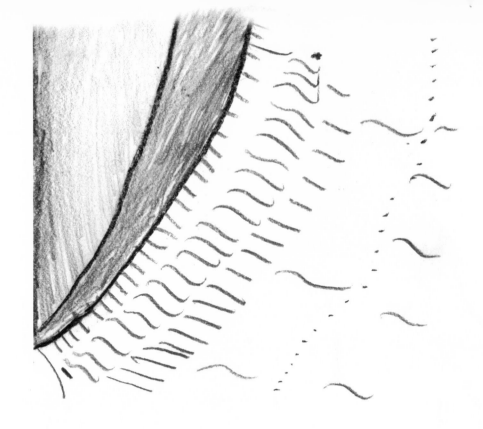

The Mother of Love

Love cannot pronounce anything
without you. You teach love how
to talk and do things.

You are the mother of love and
that means you are the mother of
everything.

You are our mother.
You are the mother of love
so within you,
you are love.

The Wings of Love

I love you so much,
my love spreads
like wings of butterflies
opening across the sky
and giving you a glorious sight
of how love can roll and turn
into beauty,
as love stretches out its arms
over the deep mountains
of wisdom.

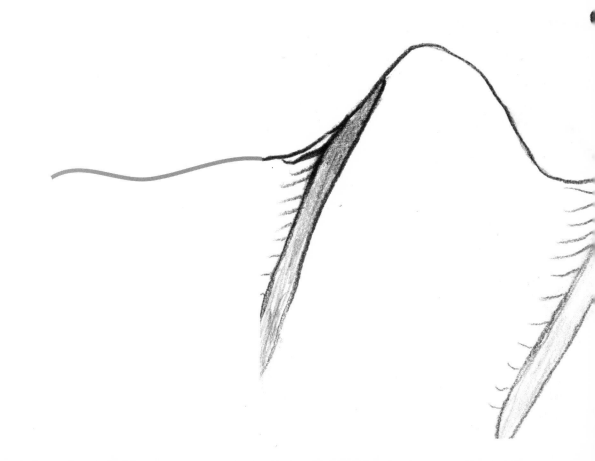

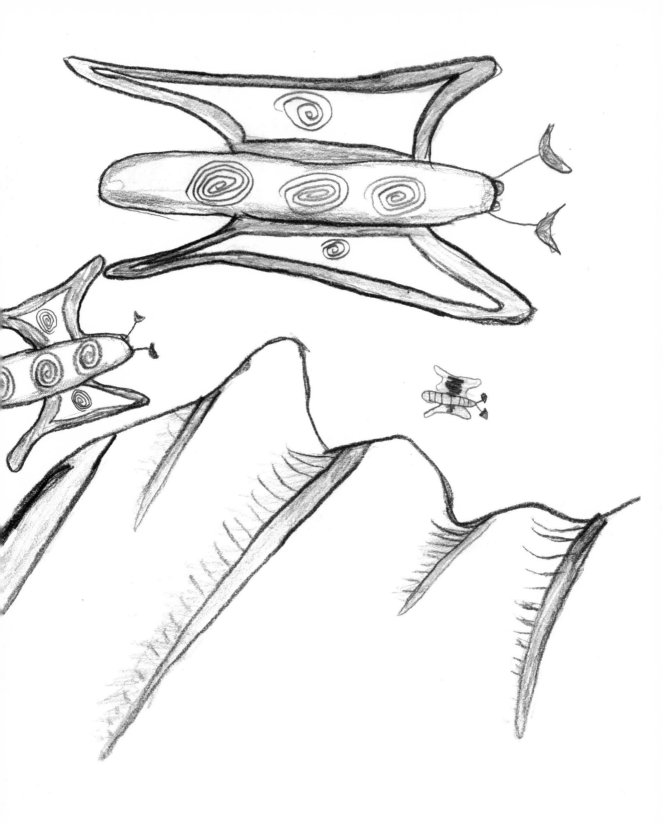

Love Saves the Day

Every person in the world,
is too dark,
without love.

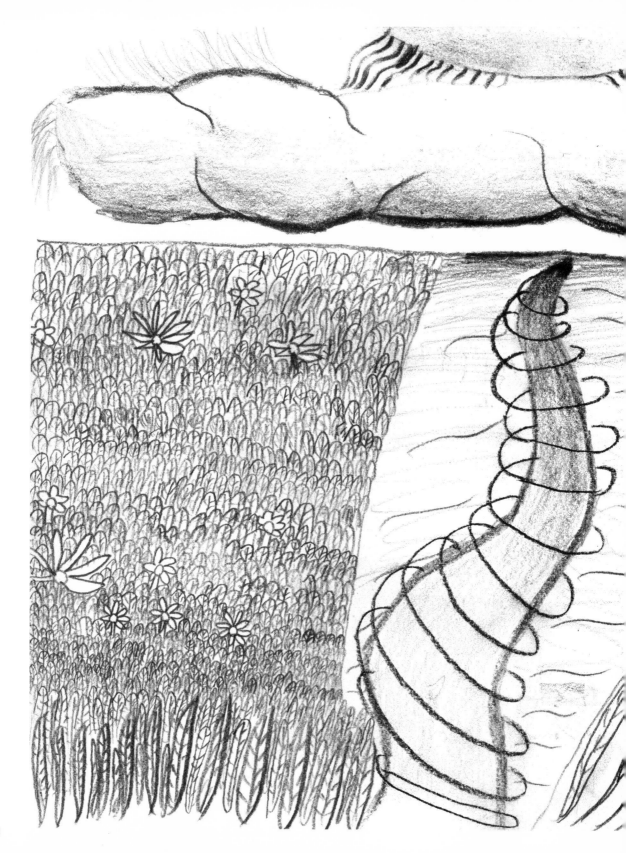

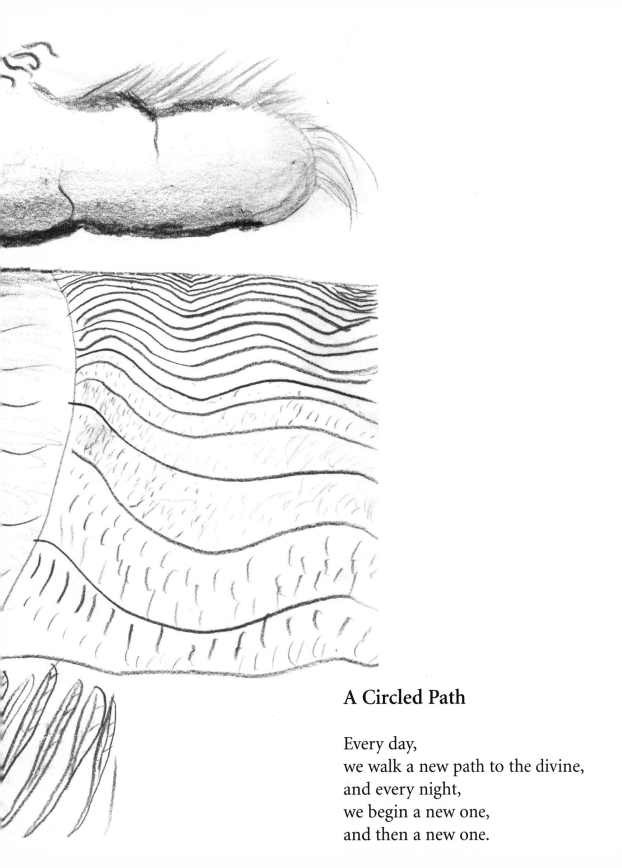

A Circled Path

Every day,
we walk a new path to the divine,
and every night,
we begin a new one,
and then a new one.

Loveliness

Wings of a falcon
fly like silk upon the beauty
within the love of our hearts.

We dance upon a daisy field,
like horses jumping over ponds,
like one single flower,
opening and blooming.

Until it reaches its part,
where it blossoms,
into a new world of loveliness.

Love's Family

There is one family that never dies.
Love's father,
Love's mother,
Love's sister,
Love's brother,
And Love.

Love and the Mountain

Love tries to climb a mountain.
It jumps and twirls,
then forms a continuous,
and endless circle,
until it reaches the top.

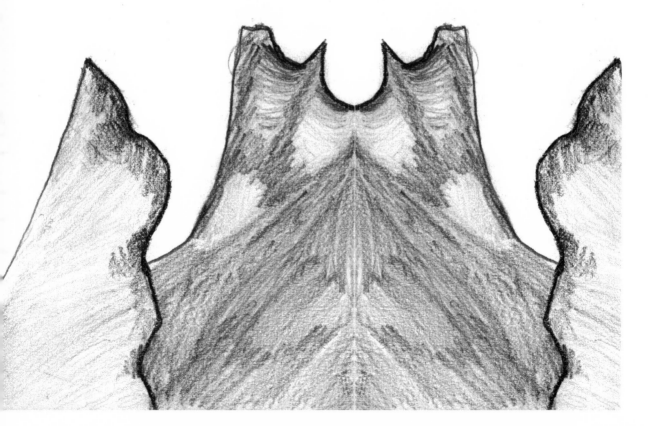

I Count on You

I count on you,
to fly with me through the sky,
and bring me to gleaming angels.
I count on you,
to flow with my heart,
into the world.
I count on you,
to go into the sky,
and put the stars out.
I count on you,
to bring the sun and moon,
into the sky
You are my angel.
We count on each other,
to bring everything to the world,
of peace and beauty.

Love Can Be Something

Love is something,
that touches your heart.
With love you get along
with friendships,
And love can be spirits and
imaginative stuff.
It can be something more
than you really know.
Love changes your activities and
gives new ones,
It makes your heart flow
with love upon your body.

poems from my heart

2000

Fishes, Trees, and Earth

Why do fishes tails swim?
Is it because they love water?
Why do trees blow?
Is it because they
love the wind?
Why do birds fly?
Is it because they
get along with the air?
Is the earth full of life
because it gets along
with something
we can only hear
within our hearts?

To All the Wild Birds

If there were frogs
with wings to fly,
Then there could be
a hummingbird that once
could cry,
I would say
to the hummingbird—
give your wings to me
and in return
I'll give you the nectar
of a lovewood tree.
And give you the pollen
from the honey flower—
I'll make sure
your nest is nice and neat,
and all your family
has lots to eat.

Worry Not

A fire
can go down
to a flame
and still
burn as bright,

A river
can go down
to a puddle
and still be
as blue
as the ocean.

A pearl
can shrink
but it is still a pearl.

A human heart can
move and grow
but we are still
human.

And the heart
still stays
inside us.

What Tears Can Do

I went up to my bed
and I lay there crying.
I sobbed in tears
and they formed a stream
in the folds of my sheet.
My eyes were wet,
as I held Teddy close.

I decided I needed love.
Love of the moon, love
of the sun, love
of birth, love
of death, love
of the eyes that
blinked once
to write poetry
then looked up
and thought
of the best soul
that could reach the Earth.

I sat up in my bed
and I decided
to become
the Goddess of the River.

I walked into the river
made from my own tears.
I went into the water
becoming
the rolling stream.

If There Would Be No Light

If there was
no sun,
there would be
no
day
to
awaken
us.

If there was
no sun,
there would be
no day
to
look
upon
us.

If there was
no moon,
there would be
no sleep
to
fall
upon
us.

If there was
no moon
there would be
nobody

to guard
our sleep.

If there were
no stars
on the nights
that there would be
no moon,
we would fall
into
a
startled
darkness.

If there were
no stars
the beauty
of angels
wouldn't
show.

If there would be
no light,
we would fall
into an
endless sleep of dust
and become
the stars,
the moon
the endless
burning sun.

Inner Self

I lay upon the greatness
of the flowing sea
in the palm of my hand.

My heart swings
with agitation
and I fly
within the boundaries
of my heart.

And I meet with you,
my angel of my wisdom . . .
my heart,
my everything.

You swing
upon the branches of my heart,
that swing out into the trees,
and the seashell yet twinkles,
not with the sand of the sea,
but with the sound of you,
whispering to me
through that seashell.

Dear Angel,
Why shall you lay on the sand?
And you are like a rock
as the sea crashes
up against you.

See what a blue jay can do—
We are the sea—
We have the sea
within our hand—
for our hand
is like a seashell,
dripping in the morning dew,
to hear the sea,
and yet we go across the sea.

Angels lighting our path
within the night.
You dance upon a light
of the only spring
that evolved out of nature.

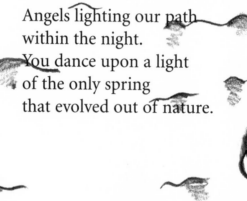

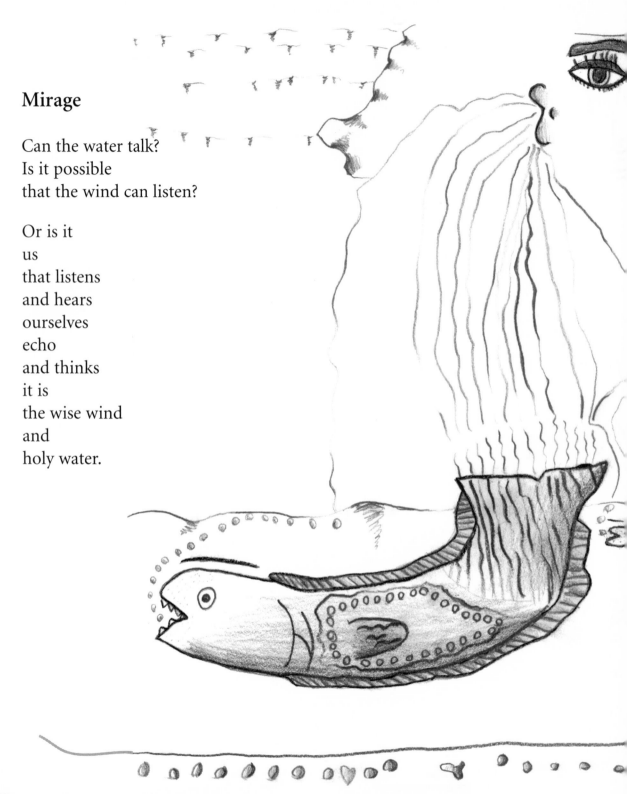

Mirage

Can the water talk?
Is it possible
that the wind can listen?

Or is it
us
that listens
and hears
ourselves
echo
and thinks
it is
the wise wind
and
holy water.

Awaken to Morning

Let love open your soul,
and awaken you
when the day has begun.
Let the morning's love open
your heart and wake you up.

With the morning's
dripping dew drops
falling gently
upon your face,
and with the morning's
sweet air, swiftly opening,
your gentle eyes.

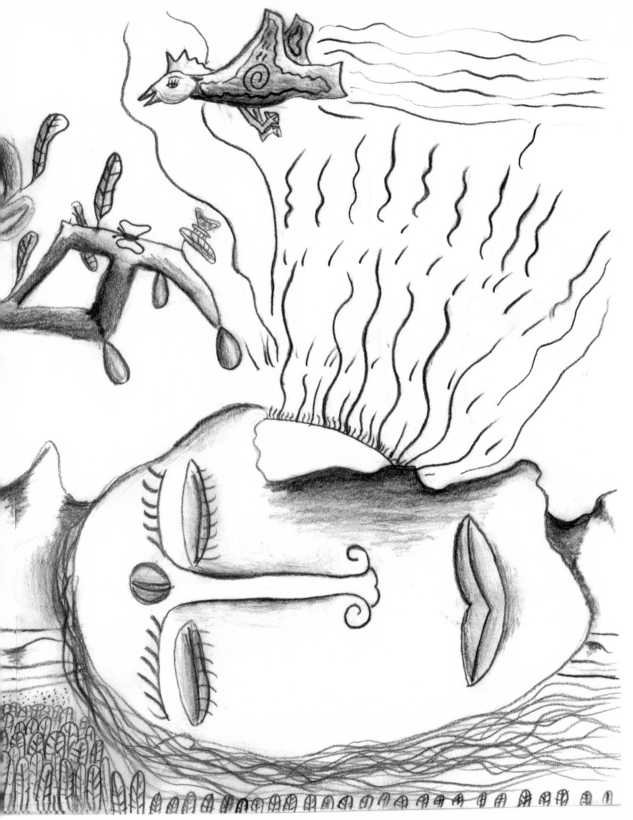

Rushing Water and My Relationship with Love

If rushing water
can hold love out,
then I will let love
come in with me.
Because if rushing water
does not want love,
I do.
And if no one will take love
in for the night,
I will.

Compared Love

The sea
holds less love than your heart.
The water
holds less faith than your soul.
And the flowing seven seas
are less
than yourself.

Love's Conversation

If you can only speak love,
then only love
can come out of your mouth.
If that is so,
then let's have a conversation
of only
love.

Meditate to Love

If we love,
be love,
If we sing,
be the sacred song.
If we need help,
be the help that you need.
If we are scared,
listen to this;
We have the strength to meditate
And by that,
you frighten everything,
that was frightening
you away.

My Soul, Love, and Peace

My soul
is only made
out of love,
so I cannot resist
burning it.

My heart
is only made
out of peace,
so I cannot resist
the peace
in the hearts
of others.

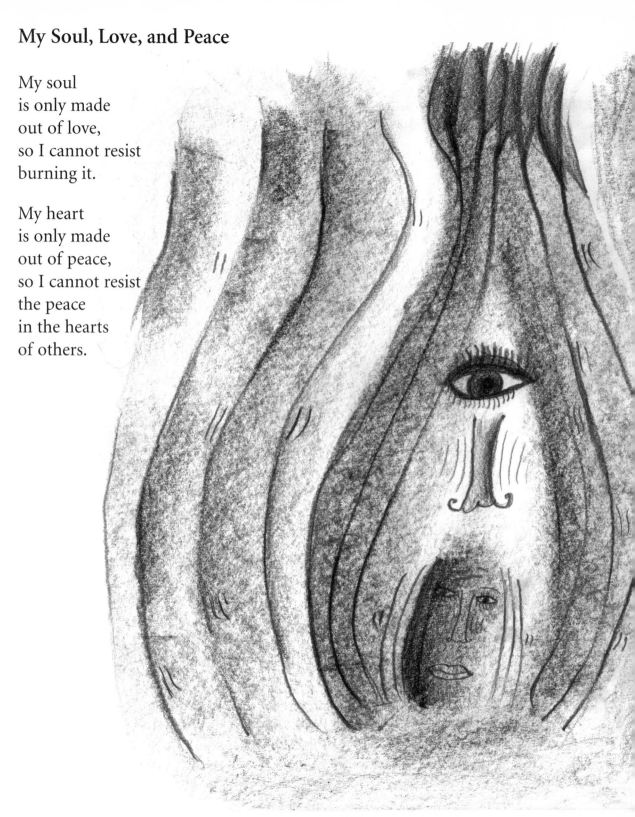

The Reminder

A baby deer
does sleep so fond
in the distant eye of the stars,
waiting to rise up to heaven.
And when it wakes,
it will be
in a peace-land of love
where no one can ever
kill it.

Your baby has a tender heart
like an angel breathing
in the midnight past tense.

Much like two angels
singing like little
nightingales
in the beauty of
a tender
life.

The wind is like a wave
crashing up against me,
like an empty satisfaction
rolling up against my body.

I am like a plant,
with my feet in the soil.
The soil,
which makes life grow
as if it were wet
but not wet at the same time.

Two hours will pass
as nature fills my heart
with things I might have to say
about the earth.

Nature Girls

Girls spin life
because they are the makers
of it.
Girls are mother nature,
because mother nature
was once a girl.
Girls are the sun
because they are bright
and shiny.
Girls are the moon
because they give us
good dreams.
Nature is full of girls and
girls are full of life,
because girls are nature
and girls have life.

Swing to Me

Swing my heart,
to love.
Swing the branches
to the trees.
Swing the air,
to my nose,
so I can breathe.
Swing to beauty.
Swing to faith.
Swing into a sacred journey,
Swing to me.

Spring

The prettiest flower
I ever saw
are the petals of your hair
and the opening bud
of your face.
My beautiful heart
is the flower
of my living
soul.
Your powerful life
are the hands
of your touching
heart.

Love's Dream

I love the only love
in Love's dream.
I wouldn't dream of hating
any hatred in the world.
We must be for love.
We all have beauty within us.
We must bow to peace
and do it correctly.
For there is
something within us,
that will never refuse
love, peace and beauty.

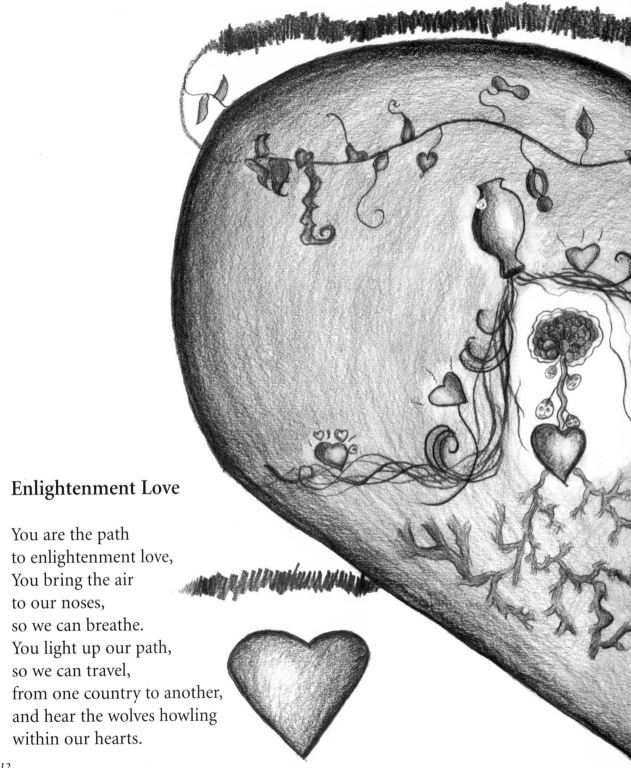

Enlightenment Love

You are the path
to enlightenment love,
You bring the air
to our noses,
so we can breathe.
You light up our path,
so we can travel,
from one country to another,
and hear the wolves howling
within our hearts.

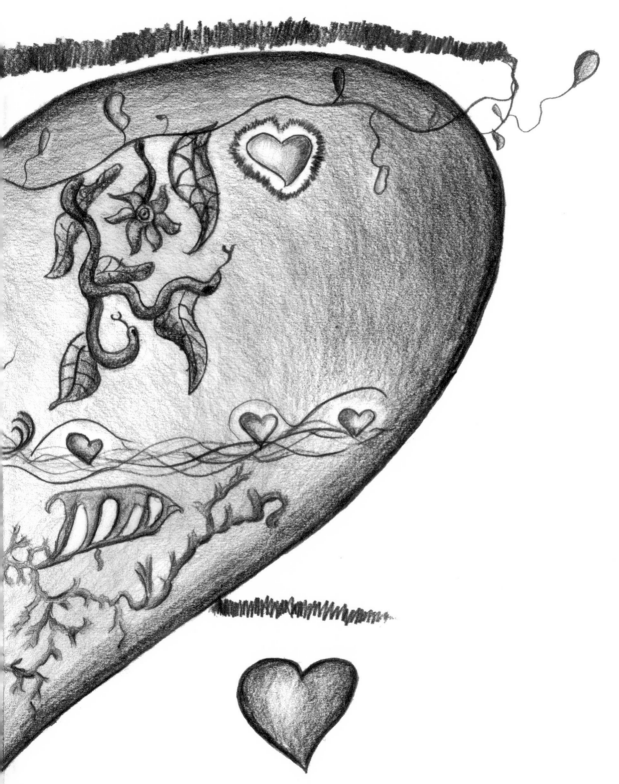

Thank you

I thank Gloria Steinem for inspiring me with poems for girls.

And my thanks to the wonderful teachers, staff, and students of the Nueva School for their encouragement and support.

I thank Mark Lemley of Copy Central for making careful, beautiful first prints of all the poetry books.

And I thank Amy Thomas, president of Pegasus Book Store for buying my first homemade copies and providing a good experience for me.

And thanks to Liz Perle, my editor, for recognizing my work.

And thank you to my mommy for exposing me to the arts and inspiring my heart with poems. And thank you for helping me to erase all my smudggies and setting up my drawing table.

Fin